CRITICAL THINKING

A Beginner's Guide To Critical Thinking, Better Decision Making and Problem Solving!

Jenifer Wilson

Contents

Chapter 7: How to Sharpen Your Skills in Decision Making

Unique Techniques of Honing Decision Making Skills
How to Ensure Your Decisions Are Foolproof
Techniques to Help Refine Your Decisions

Chapter 8: Using Questioning in Critical Thinking

General Benefits of Asking Questions
How to Design Questions to Enhance Critical Thinking

Chapter 9: Critical Thinking Strategies

Key Strategies to Make You Great At Critical Thinking

Chapter 10: The Need to Think Logically

How to Improve and Enhance Logical Thinking

Chapter 11: The Make-Up of a Skilled Critical Thinker

Attributes of Great Critical Thinkers
How to Assess the Worthiness of Views
Understanding Cycles of Consciousness
The Need to Learn Some New Skill
Learning To Write For Reading
Going Through Aromatherapy
Taking User Friendly Drugs
Keeping Your Brain Active and Busy

Chapter 12: How to Develop 5 Critical Thinking Types

Critical Thinker's Modes of Thinking
How to Develop Fundamental Leadership Skills
Thinking versus Feeling
Nature of a Critical Thinking Mindset
How the Best Managers Make Decisions
Decision Making Tips the Best Managers Follow
Ways to Incorporate Your Evidence into Decision Making

Conclusion

Introduction

Do you know your brain works like a computer? In fact, your brain, which is actually a 3-pound mass, is a natural supercomputer that acts as your body's command center. It is central to the workings of your body's every part just the same way as it is involved in whatever you do in your life. It is the part of your makeup that determines how your thoughts flow, how you direct your actions and also what your social disposition is like. It is actually the same brain that regulates what kind of person you become, controlling your thoughtfulness, your politeness, your degree of rudeness, how you handle dangerous situations and even how you conduct yourself with strangers, colleagues, family and friends.

It is right to say your brain is in charge of your emotional wellbeing. It is also influential in how you relate to people of the opposite gender. Essentially, what you need to know is that your brain is involved in virtually everything that you are involved in throughout your life. That is the reason you need to take care of it, feed it, exercise it and understand how it works, if you are to succeed in polishing your creative thinking skills. Needless to say, only when you are able to handle critical thinking are you in a position to solve problems and handle challenging situations in a way that makes things better for you and those you intend to assist.

Your brain is actually more complex than a computer. For example, the brain happens to have 100 billion nerve cells, and all the nerve endings happen to have connections with many other cells. You may find it hard to believe but that same brain you may think is not very big has many more connections within it than the number of stars there are in the universe. Physical connections notwithstanding, just be informed that you become the best you can be in your workplace, in matters of relationship, in recreation, and all other areas, when you put effort in optimizing your brain function.

When it comes to exercising, your brain's needs as much exercise as your physical body does. That is why some people choose to regularly lift weight, do yoga, consume healthy foods and do other things that are geared towards improving the health of the brain. Often the way your brain works can signal how your soul is doing, as it is that brain that gives shelter to the computer that runs your life. It actually does not matter what your age is. The fact is that your brain needs to be exercised, and when you exercise it regularly, the positive effect is manifested in your life. In summary, when you want your brain to remain capable of solving problems, including challenging ones, you need to take care of it, both in what you feed it and how regularly you exercise it.

This book, *"Critical Thinking: A Beginner's Guide To Critical Thinking, Better Decision Making and Problem Solving!"* discusses critical thinking that includes smart strategies and logical thinking. It also discusses the best decision making skills you need to acquire. Everything discussed in the book calls for reasoning at a very high level, which means your brain must, out of necessity, be in tiptop shape. It is for this reason that this book explains what you need to do to exercise your brain, and what you can do to become a logical thinker. You will also learn from this book the best techniques to sharpen your decision-making skills.

Chapter 1: Critical Thinking in Plain Terms

Have you ever thought that critical thinking can help you to be objective? It actually can. To appreciate this, bear in mind the fact that whenever you are engaged in critical thinking, you are not going to respond to something instantaneously. Instead, when you hear something, whether it is a question or a statement, you are going to ensure you heard it right. Then you will proceed to assess what it could actually mean in the context it was said. Only then will you be set to make a decision depending upon whether it is something you can believe or relate to or not. What you will eventually see is that after evaluating all the different sections of what you have listened to, and you have had opportunity to consolidate the different meanings, the conclusion you come to is normally one that is reasonable and objective.

How to Structure Your Critical Thinking Process

- Pick out the distinct ideas in the material you are trying to assess

- Check how those ideas relate to one another, or how they contrast against one another

- Assess the relevance of every idea, and also its importance

- Identify the distinct arguments in the material you have, and proceed to assess how much weight each one of them bears

- Now create arguments that demonstrate how far you agree with specific arguments as presented, and also look how far you differ with any of the ideas or arguments

- Take note of any inconsistency your find within the arguments presented. If you find any obvious misstatements, extract them so they are seen as such.

- Suggest a solution for any shortcoming you identify

- Summon your personal values during your analysis, so that they are reflected as you design your arguments to counter those that you differ with.

After speaking of distinct ideas and evaluating their veracity, can you now see there is no way you can argue out of ignorance? To pass the test of critical thinking, your arguments must be glaringly different from what is passed on along a gossip thread. Yours must, of necessity, be supported by facts from start to finish.

Something else you need to note when considering critical thinking is that having knowledge is not sufficient. You should be in a position to put the events you know about, and other facts that you know, in a logical arrangement, and you need to be pretty clear of what point you are putting where, and the reason for it. The point here is that in your critical thinking, you need to have the competency to analyze data and real issues in a manner that makes sense of the information you have. Once you are able to put what you know in the right perspective, the knowledge you have can serve a more superior cause.

Why Critical Thinking Is Important

As you have just seen, your critical thinking helps you to contribute to a higher cause using the knowledge you have. You can now look at the points that follow, to see how this process helps.

- You get to note any arguments that have no basis

- You get to note any fallacies contained in the information

- You get to introduce objective arguments

- You get to strengthen any objective arguments already presented with additional facts

- You get a chance to beef up the good arguments with logical arguments

- You get a chance to contribute positively to the tasks you find constructive

- You get opportunity to improve on existing theories

- You get opportunity to improve on the mode of operation in place

- You get opportunity to modify the way institutions run, and to enhance their strong points.

In essence, therefore, any time your knowledge is needed and it is important that it is analyzed and assessed with objectivity, critical thinking comes in handy.

Does Critical Thinking Hinder Creativity?

No, it doesn't. On the contrary, many critical thinkers are adept at thinking beyond the norm, beyond the surface, beyond the scope ordinary folk may think or essentially thinking outside the box. That is, without dispute, being creative, innovative and probably even adventurous with your imagination. In short, the fact that you are called upon to use logic when thinking critically does not disqualify you from being creative. What you cannot afford to be, even with your imagination working freely, is reckless. Instead, you evaluate points, and if they do not make sense under the circumstances, you let them go.

Fruits of Critical Thinking

Streamlining thinking

By streamlining what is meant is giving your thinking direction. You will appreciate how important this is when you consider that you, very likely, do not have the monopoly of certain information on which you are basing your arguments. As such, it is what you have as your values and your level of competence as a critical thinker that determine the kind of argument you come up with, and how helpful that argument will be to all involved.

Or do you think legal experts lose cases because they have inadequate information? For most part, this isn't the case. Often, one party is better at critical thinking than the other, or personal values of one party are at loggerheads with those of the jury, and thus the two sides cannot concur – same information, same statutes, yet different arguments and varying deductions.

The same logic is in play in other fields such as business, policymaking and so on. When serious decisions are to be made, research is conducted in order to gather data and information. It is analyzed within the perimeter of critical thinking, and then final decisions are made.

Helping to improve the global economy

When you are dealing with market forces today and resources that are available, and also the locations where those resources are found, you need to have the data available that is well analyzed in order to form useful information. Critical thinking is central to this process, otherwise you would have resources underutilized, others over-employed and yet others misused. With critical thinking, for example, you get to determine whether it is viable to put up a factory in one location or another, and if it is economical to use labor-intensive methods of production as opposed to mechanical based processes.

Such basic considerations can lead to you putting up an industry in Country A as opposed to Country B, and even exporting products to Country B instead of another country. Mark you, critical thinking pre-supposes you are ready with enough information to help you make decisions, or that you are going to do the necessary research in that regard and know what criteria you need to explore.

Have you noted the implication here that you do not use crude data for your decision-making? This cannot happen where critical thinking is involved. In fact, it would be taking too much risk in business, in politics and even in your personal life, to purport to use information in its crude form. For that reason, it is important that in big projects, you have a team of people analyzing the information at hand, and doing it in an appropriate context, so that the information is put to good use. Why else do you think institutions that think big form think tanks?

Something else worth noting is that critical thinking calls for you not only to be equipped with adequate information, but also to be broader in your thinking. This is the era of technology, remember? And you can seize great opportunities at a global level if you do your critical thinking right, whatever your specialty is. Being able to search and communicate globally helps you with your timing; whether you are looking at export opportunities, favorable import prices, more suitable immigration rules or anything else. And all these process are part of the critical thinking process.

Helping to enhance efficiency in communication

In critical thinking, you get to organize data in a way that gives a sensible picture of something or a situation, one that helps you to form an opinion, and even make a decision based on that picture. In critical thinking, you also get to analyze and assess data, with a view to forming a well thought out opinion regarding the situation. In short, you can only present an idea with valid arguments when you have been engaged in critical thinking.

Enhancing creativity

Do you ever imagine that creativity begins and ends with organizing colors and patterns to form a captivating picture? Well, it does not. It extends far beyond that, including being able to organize ideas in different ways, and then assessing what each set of ideas reflects. You can use some crude analogy to bring this point home, of the idea of eating and the idea of living. Depending on how you organize those two ideas, you could be living to eat or eating to live. Do you realize how differently you would tailor your life in each case? The basic point here is that critical thinking will drive you to digging up more ideas, discarding some ideas and also adopting others. All this thinking, and weighing of ideas, ends up sharpening your creativity in a significant way.

Promoting self reflection

As you engage in critical thinking, you gauge every move you want to make in advance, and weigh up its pros and cons. And since you are intent on having a fruitful life, you consider the option you have in all spheres of your life. Only after reasonable comprehensive assessment do you choose the root to follow. Of course, your values come into play all the while. So, inevitably, self-reflection cannot be skipped whenever you are engaging in critical thinking.

Providing a solid foundation for any scientific findings and development

Here, we are talking of a field that deals with facts and precise data, and not assumptions and generalizations. As such, critical thinking is unavoidable if you are to make any headway in science. Scientists are actually known to develop theories after serious critical thinking, and the theories and principles they come up with end up standing the test of time. Think of the Law of Buoyancy, the Law of Reflection, the Oxygen Theory of Combustion and such other theories.

Providing grounds for democracy

Well, without introducing politics into the issue of critical thinking, you will appreciate that being able to make an informed choice of your own volition is part of democracy. In fact, how can one contend there is democracy at work, for instance, if information is not being disseminated in its correctness, in whole, and in a timely manner to those engaged in voting? How, also, can anyone conclude there is democracy at work, if the environment is not conducive to questioning the data provided, or even to check the veracity of the information given? In short, whenever critical thinking is enabled, democratic space is created and people involved are happy to make informed choices.

It is such a process that helps to root out politicians who are opportunists and give chances to politicians of vision, those willing to sincerely serve their voters. It is also such a process of critical thinking that allays people's baseless fears, some of which may result from general biases and prejudices.

Chapter 2: How to Develop Skills in Critical Thinking

How would you sum up critical thinking? Some scholars like Michael Scriven and Richard Paul have said it is that process that calls for intellectual discipline in actively and also skillfully conceptualizing and applying, and also analyzing and synthesizing, plus evaluating information, which you will then use to guide you to your beliefs, and also toward choosing your course of action. According to these scholars, the information you use in the critical thinking process will comprise that you will have generated or gathered or even observed, experienced, reflected upon, reasoned about, or even communicated.

In common parlance, what these scholars have said is that critical thinking is some active process that uses varying skills whenever there is a problem to be solved. Those skills are what you are going to read about as you proceed with this chapter. What you need to understand, for the moment, is the fact that you need to employ critical thinking on a daily basis. In fact, as long as there is a problem to be solved, or there is a decision to be made from among two or more options, you have no choice but to think critically. It is the only way you can succeed in your endeavors.

Importance of Critical Thinking

According to the ancient English philosopher, Francis Bacon, critical thinking is that desire that you have to seek, the patience you have to doubt, the fondness with which you meditate, the slowness by which you assert, the readiness with which you consider, the carefulness with which you dispose of something as you set others in order, and the hatred you have for anything that can pass as an imposter.

As you digest that explanation, let us cite a few examples to show how important critical thinking is. You can actually see its importance in:

- The way it helps you to communicate effectively

- The precision with which it helps you solve problems

- The inevitability of analyzing matters and making choices in everyday tasks such as driving, preparing some academic or professional presentation, and so on

Basics of Developing Skills in Critical Thinking

Is there any success story you know that has no foundation? Likewise, if you are to succeed in critical thinking, you have got to know the basics of how to go about it. Here are the skills you need to hone:

Keen observation

What are you observing? How did you see it begin, proceed and end? Any hitches you observed? Being able to watch and take in what is happening is very important for accuracy of information, for the sake of being able to note which happenings are dependent on others, and such other solid reasoning.

You would be right to define observation as what you do without utilizing any tools, to enable you perceive information pertaining to your surroundings, or even regarding some subject.

Observation is central to any analytical process, and it is actually what you do first and foremost. As a matter of fact, human beings keep observing things and happenings around them, sometimes just accidentally and, at other times, as a deliberate move in their critical observation.

The Art of Observation within Varying Fields
Passive observation

Any idea what passive observation means? Well, it is what you do casually almost every minute that you are awake. It means what you register with your common senses on a continual basis, without even planning on it. You see, varying colors borne by objects around you, shapes as well, you register different scents and sometimes odors, you feel varying textures with your hands or other parts of your body and you even notice moving objects changing speed, and the environment changing temperature.

All those observations can be made casually, or they can be a result of an exercise you have deliberately planned to undertake – spontaneous observation, or observation as part of critical thinking, where you may wish to collect information for the sake of carrying out some critical analysis.

Psychological observation

Observations of a psychological nature are often made during experiments or on an ordinary day in the course of natural behavior. In psychology, observations are of a visual nature, and sometimes of a vocal nature. So, essentially, you utilize video and other devices that record sound, as tools to help in observing and analyzing those observations.

Meteorological observation

In the field of meteorology, you use specialized tools to make observations regarding the weather elements. Here, we are talking of observing changes in temperature, matters regarding atmospheric pressure, degree of precipitation and humidity and also the intensity and speed of wind. Observations are actually very crucial in this field, as the basis of extensive and in-depth analysis.

Medical observation

The medical field, just like the meteorological field, depends heavily on the observations made. In this field, observations are made for the sake of making a diagnosis and deciding the appropriate treatment. Here, tools are utilized to take note of the patient's heart rate, the blood pressure, the body temperature and so on. Once this wide range of data is collected through observation, it is then used to determine the next medical course of action with regard to the patient being observed.

Experience

You can take experience as the strongest pillar among the skills of critical thinking, and this is because it is the experiences in your personal life that often influence the direction of your critical thinking process. These experiences include things you discovered when you were very young, and things you experienced only this morning.

Take the example of a child painting a home chair from his color palate. As he does this, he gets to learn some universal truths, like the way a painted surface looks. If his mother admonishes him for painting his chair, he gets to learn that people can get upset when you interfere with their items without permission.

How about when you are doing cooking in the kitchen and washing the dishes? Are there not some principles that you learn during these processes that help in critical thinking? You learn how ceramics respond to heat as opposed to how glass items do, which helps you later when analyzing situations in critical thinking. You also cannot underrate the lessons you learn from the experiences you go through in your adolescence. They do, inevitably, influence your critical thinking skills.

Incidentally, even your own personality can be influenced somewhat by your experiences. For instance, if a ridiculous pose by your kid during a photo session gets people laughing, the child may get into the habit of pulling that stunt whenever he wants to catch attention. All your experience may come in handy in helping your critical thinking, but what seems to play the biggest role in molding and sharpening your critical thinking skills is your interpersonal experience. Why do you think this is the case? Well, you get to learn what to anticipate from other people when you behave in a certain way, and also how you are bound to react when other people behave in a given way. These experiences influence the way you behave, and although you need more than experience to develop strong critical thinking skills, these experiences are the most convenient ways of learning fresh skills in critical thinking.

Reflection

When you give serious consideration to something, or what you can call giving serious thought, you can term that as reflection. Reflection is actually necessary in critical thinking. You cannot just take things and happenings as you see them, without giving them due consideration or thought. You may have observed something happen, for instance, and you actually lived through the experience, but for you to form a reliable opinion, you have got to consider the circumstances under which the event happened, the people who were involved, the probability that whatever happened could have been changed, and such other factors.

Here, your reflection would be helping your mind to process your experiences, and sieving through the relevant parts from those experiences that are irrelevant in your decision-making. You must be able to reflect on things for you to be able to reason about events, and to be able to communicate those happenings correctly to other people. The reality is that reflection influences the way you perceive yourself, as well as the way you perceive the world in general. You also need to note that others involved in these experiences may have a different viewpoint that is equally valid.

Reasoning

Reasoning is how you think and how you understand issues so that you are able to derive conclusions or make judgments. Reasoning is based on logic, and it is also based on available evidence.

Even when you are learning in school, you appreciate things better when you can reason, because you can go through facts and supporting evidence and come to a logical conclusion as to why things happen in a certain way, or why things in the past happened as they did. It is reasoning that helps you decide what to take in as important in your life, and what to relegate to the back burner. It supports your critical thinking process, leading you to gathering your different thoughts as well as any information you have, in preparation to taking any steps you may deem necessary. In short, reasoning helps you to have a better understanding of the issue at hand.

Now, are you always reasoning the same way? Of course, not! The way you reason will, most likely, depend on the facts you have, the circumstances in which things happened and so on. So, you will see reasoning categorized differently as in:

Moral reasoning

Here, it is your moral standard that comes into play, and you use that to come to a conclusion regarding the matter at hand.

Inductive reasoning

Here, you take some particular information, and from that information you make some general conclusions.

Deductive reasoning
In this category of reasoning, it is the general information that you use, to make conclusions of a specific nature. Whatever form of reasoning you apply, the point is that you are trying to come to conclusions regarding a certain issue.

Would you like examples of times when reasoning is called into play?
Here:

On a daily basis
Surely we don't use logic on a daily basis to solve issues that come up in the course of our work and in other areas of our life. In fact, you do. Even the people we come into contact with call for us to reason. If you think about it seriously, the ideas some of those people come up with are obnoxious, and some people often have questionable morals. Under those circumstances, only your ability to reason can help you make the most appropriate decisions, such as to how to relate to each of these people, and also what ideas of theirs to adopt and which ones to ignore.

In the course of business
Have you noticed that many employers are impressed by employees who can reason? That is one factor they look for when conducting job interviews. They want employees who are capable of drawing conclusions from given facts and scenarios. This is important for the employees to be able to take decisions that are geared towards taking advantage of business opportunities, and even decisions geared towards protecting the business brand. Decision makers need less supervision.

In the field of sports

When it is practice time or the time of the real game, a sports team takes its time to thoroughly think through how they are going to approach the game and tackle it, and they do this by taking into account the competence or assumed skills of their opponents. In short, the team must reason as to the best moves to take, and in what form or order, so as to finally beat the rival team.

Communicating

You can take communicating to be the exchange of thoughts as well as information between parties. Is this not what you do almost on a continuous basis? Although you may have taken that for granted, you may appreciate that serious topics tend to go smoothly whenever you have thought critically about what to say before actually saying it. In fact, there is one saying of the wise that alleges it is important to *think before you speak.*

If you want to be a great communicator:

- Taking thinking deeply seriously

- Take other people's perspectives into consideration

Only after doing this are you confident you are giving a response that is warranted at the time and under the circumstances that prevail.

Take away lessons from this chapter

What you need to take away from this chapter is that it is important to be fair in your assessment of situations, and it is also important that you be rational in your decision-making. This is useful in your career, in business, in your social life and virtually everywhere. Finally, all the skills of critical thinking are very important to your success and to the way in which other people see you. If, for example, as a manager, you suspect that one of your employees is pilfering stuff from what you have observed, and also from your personal experience about how people tend to behave when they are siphoning stuff from the business, you do not just reflect on what you suspect and reason about what the implications of retaining or not retaining the employee are. You are also able communicate your thoughts to that employee.

Otherwise, if you miss one step, such as communicating, and you just sign the employee's letter of dismissal, how would you ever know if there was another employee purposely sabotaging this particular employee? Without effective communication, how would the other managers and employees be sure you fired this employee on fair grounds?

Your skills combine observation, given facts, input from all sources and your experience and ability to handle each situation based on your own critical thinking powers.

Chapter 3: Alternate Ways of Sharpening Critical Thinking

What Critical Thinking Is

You have seen a lot in the previous chapter about how to go about thinking critically, but how can you describe critical thinking? You may take it to be the ability to mentally process things in a clear and rational manner, as you appreciate the logical connection existing amongst different ideas. There has been serious debate amongst scholars regarding critical thinking, and even famous philosophers like Plato and Socrates were at loggerheads in their time. Such discussions have not ceased with modern knowledge, and so it is only right that you learn something practical about critical thinking - something applicable in today's life.

You would actually be right to describe critical thinking as that ability you have to reflect on things and think about them in an independent way. Basically, for you to carry out critical thinking, you need:

- To be able to reason and to engage in active learning, as opposed to waiting to receive information as you remain passive.

- To be prepared to question ideas as well as assumptions in a rigorous manner, instead of just accepting them at face value. As a critical thinker, you are expected to make efforts to establish if the ideas and arguments before you, and any related findings as well, are representative of the whole picture. As you do this, it is important that you be open to finding out what you did not expect as well as what you did expect.

- To be in a position to identify and analyze problems, all in a systematic way. In short, in critical thinking, you do not base your decisions on mere intuition or opinion. You do not rely solely on your instincts to make judgment.

Benefits of Having Critical Thinking Skills

- Understanding the links existing amongst various ideas

- Being able to determine the importance of arguments and also ideas, and their relevance in the particular context

- Ability to recognize and appraise arguments, and also to design your own

- Being able to pick out inconsistencies in the reasoning, as well as any errors in the arguments made

- Ability to be systematic and consistent in the way you tackle problems

- Ability to reflect on how justified your own assumptions, values, as well as beliefs, are

You can actually summarize critical thinking as:

- Weighing issues in a way that enables you to get the best solution under the prevailing circumstances. Generally speaking, whenever you consider the things going through your mind and you weigh them, in order to pursue the best options, this is critical thinking

- Weighing specific things at a given moment, as opposed to dealing with accumulated facts. Critical thinking does not also constitute learning and evaluating facts today, and then calling on that knowledge to always help you make decisions. Critical thinking, as you have seen, takes into account changing circumstances, developing issues and such other dynamics.

To be able to carry out your critical thinking process well, you may wish to look at the necessary skills more specifically and, in this regard, you can work towards honing the skills of:

1. **Observation**

2. **Analysis**

3. **Interpretation**

4. **Reflection**

5. **Evaluation**

6. **Inference**

7. **Explanation**

8. **Problem solving**

9. **Decision making**

What we are basically saying is that in critical thinking, you are called upon to:

- Ponder over issues in an objective way and also in a critical manner

- Point out and distinguish the varying arguments within an issue

- Assess every viewpoint, to be able to tell with confidence if that perspective is valid or not, and if it is, how strong or weak it is

- Pick out any weaknesses, or what you may term negative points, in whatever evidence is being presented, or whatever argument is being made.

- See and point out the implications of every statement and every argument in the discussion at hand

- Construct support for any argument you present, making your reasoning very clear, so that anyone listening can see the basis on which you are making your statements, allegations, denunciations... whatever the gist of your argument is.

There are few things you can accomplish without practice, and in the case of critical thinking, you could hone the relevant skills through good practice. First of all, you need to appreciate that it is not always that you think critically, as in observing, analyzing, reflecting and the rest of it even when the talk is taking place in a fun situation. Even in times of anger, it is rare that you think critically. Most times you react on the spur of the moment, only to ponder over your response later. There are other times when you do not think critically, times such as when you are grieving. The process of critical thinking is interrupted by emotions.

Is it all right to react spontaneously as when in anger? Of course, most times it is not. It can cause more pain to others and to you, more than it can improve matters. So, whenever you can, it is a good idea that you learn how to improve your ability to summon and engage in critical thinking. Remember, ordinarily, your ability to think critically depends on how your mindset is at a particular moment. Thus, give yourself space between anger and action.

Routine Activities to Help You Improve Critical Thinking

Can you summon to mind something that someone recently said to you? Once you remember something like this, address these questions to yourself:

- Who actually said this?

- Was it one of the people I'm familiar with?

- Is it someone I look up to, probably a person with authority?

- Is it really important from whom this statement came?

- What are the exact words this person uttered?

- Did this person provide facts? If so, were those facts exhaustive or did the person miss out some fact(s)?

- Where was this person at the time of speaking?

- Did this person utter the words in public place, or was it in private?

- Did anyone else provide input or offer an alternative observation or view?

- When did this person utter the words?

- Was this before some important event, during the event, or afterwards?

- Is the timing of this statement significant?

- Why did this person make the utterance?

- Did the person provide an explanation as to why he/she told you whatever it was you learned? Were they, for whatever reason, out to make somebody look bad or look good? What was their motive?

- How was the emotional balance of the person when making the statement – annoyed, sad or indifferent? Did the person write down or simply say the statement? Did you actually understand fully the statement that the person made?

Establishing What You Want to Achieve

When you want to do farming, you do not just send the plough to the farm and find that the next thing you are doing is digging furrows. You need to establish what it is you want to plant, and how far apart you want your rows to be. In short, you will be making an important decision on the basis of multiple possibilities. In other words, you will be defining your aim on the basis of a range of possible actions. Needless to say, if your aim is to cultivate beans you are likely going to make your furrows closer than if your aim was to grow maize. In case your aim is to farm Irish potatoes, you may even choose to dig some extra rounds with the harrow, in order to make the soil finer before planting.

This analogy goes to show how important it is to define your aim before you begin the critical thinking process. In any case, factors that may be favorable and wanted in one situation may be unfavorable and unwanted in a different situation.

Your aim then becomes your starting point in whatever you may want to do in the future.

Any move you make, or any decision you take, should be consistent with your aim. It is even a good idea to make the people around you understand what your aim is, so that their actions do not inadvertently end up messing up your efforts and plans. That's why big companies have a mission statement. Once you have established what your intention is, you need to maintain personal discipline, so that you only do things that are consistent with your goal. This, you can continue doing, until probable circumstances change, and it becomes necessary for you to revisit the process right from the start.

Chapter 4: How to Beat Hindrances to Critical Thinking

Is there a single thing you can point to that is not threatened by obstacles? Critical thinking is, definitely, not one of them and so you need to know how to go about overcoming such obstacles. Needless to say, you cannot purport to solve a problem unless you have identified the specific problems surrounding it. Therefore, in the case of critical thinking, you need to know what it is that threatens this process. What is likely to hinder your progress as you undertake critical thinking?

Often, threats to critical thinking are six in number, and they do not have to work together. In fact, any single one of them can act to sabotage your efforts at critical thinking. However, the adage to be forewarned is tantamount to being forearmed works.

8 Hindrances to Critical Thinking

(1) Missing direction

Have you heard people say something to the effect that those who don't know where they are going never reach their destination? You will never know if you are working towards your goal unless you know what your goal is. As such, you need to articulate what your goal is, and then design a plan of action to work towards achieving that goal. Normally, once you see your plan of action well drawn out, your mind begins to work creatively and it generates very innovative ideas that are geared towards improving the problem solving skills you already have. It also begins thinking of fresh ways of tackling the problem. However, if you have no idea what you want to see done at the end of the day, you have a problem from the onset. Direction is everything.

(2) Fear of failure

When we speak of fear of failure, we have in mind fear that is related to making losses, to being wrong, to losing money, to being late and the like. So, you fear that you may not succeed in business, you may lose your investment, and you may not make it in time, and so on. Do you know the part of failing that is worst of all?

Surprisingly, it is not the actual failing that is a handicap, considering you have failed in different tasks and in different spheres of your life and you are still moving ahead in your life. The real handicap is in anticipating failure. As long as you internalize the thought of failing, you do not feel motivated, and so you are hesitant to engage in anything productive. In short, you are not eager to begin the problem solving process as long as you feel you are likely to fail at it.

(3) Fearing criticism

When people fear criticism, they also fear ridicule, and, in the same vein, fear rejection. They fear being laughed at. Often, in such cases, the people concerned fear that they may be thought dumb, or make themselves look foolish. Mostly this happens with people who are eager to be liked and to get other people's approval, including approval from people they hardly know; people they hardly care about.

Unfortunately, there is a sizeable number of people who do not reach their potential simply because they are afraid that other people might think them too ambitious. Others fail to showcase their talent and expertise, fearing that other people might dismiss their efforts as worthless. Fearing criticism and rejection leaves you on the lane of underachievers, and this is simply because you choose to play it safe as opposed to focusing on your goal. Be innovative in your thinking, and ultimately put your ideas into action, the naysayers' opinions notwithstanding.

(4) The strife to remain consistent

How can you even be creative when all you are concerned about is remaining consistent with what and how you have done in the past? It does not matter that you succeeded in the past – there is big potential in thinking over something critically, considering there are always variables that might have changed over time. The point here is that the tendency to do what you have always done, through what experts term homeostatic impulse is a great hindrance to success.

When you succumb to the urge to remain constant, effectively saying you are going to remain in your comfort zone, you end up getting stuck in a zone with no creative knack and no innovativeness. Before long, you are likely to begin rationalizing not wanting to change, and not wanting to venture out of familiar territory. In short, if you entertain homeostasis, you will be hindering progress as far as problem solving is concerned. This means you are likely to find it very difficult to succeed in business and in any other undertaking you may engage in.

(5)Passive thinking

Do you know your mind does not get creative if you remain passive as opposed to being actively involved in something? In passivity, your mind has no vitality, as it is not stimulated at all. In fact, it remains short of energy just like any of your muscles that are not physically exercised. Where you normally would have been proactive and creative, you become passive and begin doing things in a kind of automatic way.

One of the things that can make you passive is routine. For example, you get into the routine of getting up at a certain hour every morning, you do the very same chores that are you are used to doing, you meet the same people you deliberately meet with, eat your meals from the same place at the same habitual hour, then proceed to watch the same TV programs you are used to day in day out. Where, then, do you get room to be creative and experimental, when routine prevails? You literally have nothing to challenge your mind, and so you just end up becoming dull. You even become complacent and do not make any attempt to learn additional ways of doing things.

Worse still, you often get to despise anyone suggesting you

try something new, and all they say is met with a negative attitude. Soon, you begin to manifest signs of being threatened whenever someone suggests you can change the way you do things.

(6) Seeking justification

How much are you going to succeed in doing if every time you are about to make a move, you halt to explain it to the world? Yet this is something that many people do. You may excuse them once you remember that human beings are basically rational beings, but trying to justify your deeds to all and sundry is bound to make you lag behind. For your business to succeed, and for whatever other undertakings are to succeed fast, you cannot wait to formulate a good reason to give the world, and then wait for the world to give you a nod. You have got to allow yourself room to do what you deem to be fitting without seeking approval from the rest of the world. The security that you seek by trying to rationalize your deeds is a handicap to success.

(7) Enculturation

When you take everything your culture bequeaths you, and you do not care to question it, you are bound to hinder your own progress. Which culture, if you may look back keenly, does not carry beliefs and practices that are not either bare bottlenecks to progress or repugnant to justice? A good number of cultures have prejudices and blind spots, and so taking such practices at face value can be a hindrance to success. You need to ignore those gaps your culture has, set traditional biases and prejudices aside, and embrace critical thinking regardless of what culture stipulates.

The point here is that you have got to be bold enough to challenge the general standpoint and think as an individual who has an independent mind, and who can reason. If you subject ideas - as well as beliefs - to logical scrutiny, you end up purifying them, and implementing them in the form and manner that is most suitable under the circumstances.

(8) Unfavorable emotional states

Who does not value calmness when faced with a challenging situation? Yet, you may often find you are making decisions without weighing how your state of mind is processing the problem. Whenever you make a decision in anger, the facts are likely to be blurred by too much negative emotion, and so the decision may not be the most fitting for the situation. This is the case too if you are depressed at the time of making the decision. Forget that the great philosophers of old, Plato and Aristotle, held anger to be supportive of great reasoning, and the respected theologian, Martin Luther, declared he thought best when annoyed. The average person just does not do any good acting when in deep emotions such as anger and depression.

Chapter 5: Use of Critical Thinking to Tackle Challenges

It is possible you have seen the standpoint of cognitive psychologists regarding the relationship between the act of thinking and the sense of feeling. These experts defy common belief that the first thing you do when something happens is to feel or show emotions, and only after that do you begin to ponder over what happened. Cognitive psychologists do not agree that feelings come automatically, and, as such, precede all other senses. On the contrary, they hold the premise that the feelings you carry result from your own thought process, and so if you can influence your thought process, you also can change the way you feel. Essentially what is being said here is that if you think of a good outcome, you will be happy even before you have seen the results, and if you think of a bad outcome you will feel low and lose motivation even before you have begun your process.

The Emotional Power of Human Beings

You also have the power to do the following:

- Influence your feelings by controlling your thought process, and this, of course, is one way of embracing critical thinking

- Influence your attitude, so that by the end of the day you have a positive world outlook. With a positive attitude, you can make judgment without prejudice, and give room for critical thinking.

- Influence your thought process so that you are able to direct your actions accordingly, and you get your anticipated results. Practically speaking, engaging in critical thinking keeps you away from stress, because at every juncture you feel you are in control of what is happening. In fact, you can fall into depression by the mere feeling that you have lost control of what is happening in your life.

- Effectively, therefore, critical thinking is not just great for success, but it is also great for your welfare.

The question that then begs to be answered is if there is actually room for you to ever behave or act instantaneously. And the answer is in the affirmative. It is very normal, as a human being, to develop feelings, even when you have not given much thought as to how you are about to feel. Nonetheless, after studying the benefits of critical thinking, you would be expected to halt and say, "I know what feelings influence my thought process negatively and which ones have a positive influence. And so I'm choosing to influence my thought process in a way that will be fruitful, rather than allowing my feelings to run amok."

Once you are informed the way you are after reading this book, you are able to quickly dissuade yourself from acting out of raw emotions. What you often find yourself doing, and which brings harmony and success to your life, is moderating your emotions, and this you do by actively engaging in critical thinking.

Can you now say you know something worthwhile about critical thinking? All right ... however, there is a simple assessment you can do, to see if you have truly mastered the necessary skills to make you successfully undertake critical thinking.

How to Test Your Mastery of Critical Thinking Skills

Whenever you are skilled at critical thinking:

- You rely on reasoning more than you do on emotions

- You do not stubbornly stick to your viewpoint, but rather you accept that it's better to evaluate different points of view

- You listen to what other people have to say, all this with an open mind

- You are prepared to receive fresh evidence whenever you are evaluating an issue, and you are also glad to accept fresh findings as well as new explanations, irrespective of whether the phase being discussed is deeply underway and is probably nearing completion.

- You are open to reassessing the information you already have

- You are prepared to set aside personal prejudices, and also ignore any biases you ordinarily have

- You are perceptive to varying options

- You are able to avoid the temptation to hastily make conclusions, and just as hastily make judgments

Looking at these points, you may conclude that critical thinking comes easy to you, but just believe it, there are many people who do not think critically when faced with a problem that needs to be solved. As such, it is important to learn the easiest way to learn critical thinking, and also the most convenient steps to take in employing those skills.

How to Carry Out Critical Thinking Step By Step

Establish what the problem is
Why is it important for you to see what the problem is from the start? If you consider that you can employ resources addressing an issue only to discover you are following the wrong trail, you can see what a waste of resources that can be. Other times, if you do not first try to identify the problem, you end up spending a lot of your time and other resources, only to establish there was no problem in the first

place, probably just a situation misread.

Undertake to analyze the problem

Why spend time analyzing the problem you have already identified? Simple – you want to know the exact nature of the problem, the areas of your project it is affecting, its magnitude and even your capacity to handle it. It is at this stage of analysis that you determine if the problem at hand is one you can deal with as an individual, if you require some additional assistance, if it is one a problem that can be handled instantly or if it can only be tackled at a later stage in the process, and such other matters of a fundamental nature.

Think up manageable solutions

Yes, you do not just delve into solving a problem without knowing the chances your chosen method has of working. Since you are, presumably, a serious thinker, and not an amateur trying to solve a problem on a trial and error basis, you need to weigh the options you think may work in your particular situation, and then pick the best. As someone who is looking for the best output for your project, you need not shy away from consulting, if it comes to it, as it is usually helpful to have different perspectives to the problem. Brainstorming is also very helpful.

Choose the best possible solution

Even though there are many roads that lead to Rome, so to speak, it would be reasonable to choose the one that is the most cost effective and the one that has the least inconvenience – and then you would term it the best. Here, too, is a case where you are likely to have several possible solutions to a challenge, and you cannot, obviously, use all of them. So it is up to you to weigh what advantages each of them has over the others and how convenient the one with the most advantages is to apply – and then you can term it your best possible solution. Remember as you pick your best option it is necessary to take into account the prevailing circumstances.

Wind up your process

How else do you wind up your process but by implementing your best solution? You cannot possibly go on searching and comparing notes, and marveling at the wide range of choices that you have, like some people go to school and study this, and then proceed to study that and the other, and hardly get to the point of putting to use what they have learnt. Remember the starting point of this process was identifying the existing problem, and you, therefore, made it your goal to look for its solution. Now you must, of necessity, take the relevant action, to see to it that the problematic issue you pointed out has been resolved.

So, if someone were to anticipate results, would you say they should wait for a drastic change in the issue at hand? To be safe, you need to say, not necessarily. Guess what? Sometimes doctors diagnose your medical problem and, after due consideration, decide you are better off living as you are, than putting you through medication, surgery or any other medical procedure. Likewise, there are some issues that are best left as they are, because any changes to them would adversely affect more people than is the case in the prevailing situation.

In short, critical thinking can give you justification to change matters, and it can also make you see that the situation as it is remains the best possible scenario. However, even when you choose to let the issue or situation remain unaltered, you need to say as much in writing, and then state the reasons that prompted you to arrive at that conclusion. When you make your stance and reasons known, everyone concerned finds it relatively easy to accept your verdict, and to live with the situation.

Do you think solving a particular problem is the only achievement you get after engaging in critical thinking? Gladly, it is not. For starters, all the information you learn from the process of critical thinking cannot be ignored. It is wealth that you can fall back on in the future if you are faced with a similar challenge. At the same time, you come from the task with a fresh boost of confidence, mainly emanating from the fact that you understand the issue at hand from all possible perspectives. So whatever the project is about, there is no fear that something untoward can crop up and take you by surprise.

Finally, the more informed you are and the more you have practically analyzed and tested scenarios, the more resourceful you become, even to people around you. And even if there was no challenge in the foreseeable future, who says there is harm in keeping your skills sharpened and your wits about you?

Chapter 6: Keeping the Brain in Shape for Critical Thinking

Which part of your body is most involved in critical thinking? It is, of course, your brain. Although your legs may carry you to different places to do your research, it is your brain that does the problem identification, the data analysis, the evaluation and most of the other necessary tasks. Most of these are roles you cannot automate no matter how tech-savvy you are, and so you need your brain to be in tiptop shape for the work. And for your brain to be in great shape, you need to exercise it, and do it regularly.

16 Exercises to Sharpen Your Brain

(1) Do enjoyable physical exercises

Does physical exercise help your brain? Yes, it does. Without going too scientific, let us just say, something happens that triggers the generation of fresh cells in your hippocampus, a part of your brain that is very central to processing of information. This means you can reason better, doesn't it? In addition, experiments performed on mice revealed that enjoying the exercises you are doing has the effect of indirectly exercising the brain as well.

For that reason, it is advisable to engage in something that you enjoy for an exercise, so that the goodness does not end with your physical state but extends to your mental state as well. Generally what experts say is that by engaging in interesting physical exercises, probably something that you like on the same level as your hobbies, you end up, not just sharpening your mind, but also increasing your happiness.

(2) Exercise your mind

We may have credited interesting physical exercises with improving the mind, but even exercising the mind directly is possible. It is actually possible to improve different parts of your brain by getting them to work, so it is great if you can establish ways of making your brain exercise, because then you will have the brain maintaining the health of its dendrites and its nerve cells. If you are wondering the relevance of those parts – the nerve cells plus the dendrites – they are the parts of your brain that receive information, and then proceed to process it.

In this case of exercising your brain, it is fine to equate brain exercises with the exercises you do to strengthen your physical muscles; like weightlifting. Just as in weightlifting you reinstate the health of underutilized flabby muscles, in brain exercises you reinstate and improve the health of parts of your brain that are, in essence, flabby too.

In a bid to exercise your brain, feel free to experience fresh scents and tastes, and even new physical feelings. It is also a good idea to try and put to use the hand of yours that is less dominant, giving it some activities to tackle. You cannot really succeed in getting that hand to work efficiently without summoning some thinking, whether deliberately or not – and that is exercise on the part of your brain. How about coming up with new routes to take you to work? That is, definitely, taking your brain out of its comfort zone, and that is great for exercise. Other easy ways of exercising your brain include traveling to places you have not been to before, doing some artwork, and even reading one of the most challenging novels around. The idea is to engage your brain in doing something that it is not used to; something that is not routine for it.

(3) Question things

Do you know why questioning is great for your brain? It means you are prepared to search for answers. And just as you do great legwork when searching in the woods or search a vast area, you will do great exercise with your brain when searching for answers. Carrying on your childhood tendencies of trying to satisfy your curiosity is healthy for your brain, and so you need not stifle that natural trait. In fact, you need to deliberately question whatever is happening around you, in other parts of the world, or even the reason for the things that are happening in your life, or those that are affecting your life in one way or the other.

In a bid to satisfy your curiosity, you should not hesitate to consult people you believe are in the know. Experts reckon it is a good idea to make it a practice to ask why, and so it is recommended that you sort out why something like ten times or more in one day.

(4) Make a point of laughing

Do you have to listen selectively, so that you only hear things that are amusing? The answer is no. Rather, you need to be able to appreciate the light side of life. Just as they say about the silver lining of the cloud, there should, seriously, be something light about even the most serious of subjects. It does you no good at all, for instance, to frown at food as you eat; chewing as if eating is a continuation of your day job. If you behave this way, you will be tiring your brain and condemning it to a life of dullness.

On the contrary, you need to be open to amusement all the time without hesitation, because it does not inhibit your serious thinking. Instead, it catalyzes the production of endorphins by your brain, a substance often referred to as the 'happy drug.' Believe it or not, once you are happy and feeling a positive high, you are likely to be open to suggestions, and you are also likely to comprehend things better. Laughing keeps your mind active and vibrant, thus contributing positively to your success in critical thinking. Look at laughing actually as recharging the battery of your brain.

(5)Feed on Omega 3 fats

The fact that Omega 3 is great for your heart does not mean it cannot be great for other parts of the body. After all, body functions are somehow interrelated. Anyway, the Omega 3 fats do help your heart pump more amounts of oxygen to your brain, and that means better functioning of that organ. That increased supply of oxygen has actually been seen to improve the function of those membranes surrounding the brain cells. Moreover, it is even thought that consuming fish, which happens to be a good source of Omega 3, helps you keep some serious ailments away, such as dementia and depression, and also conditions such as attention deficit disorder, all of which are ailments affecting the brain.

Also, considering that essential oils are great for brain development in young ones, it is also possible that the benefit contributes to high intelligence level and improved mental state. Gladly, you can also get Omega 3 fats from eating flaxseed as well as walnuts.

(6) Take a walk down memory lane

It is good to get into the habit of remembering good times because such memories make you happy and, as you have already seen, happiness stimulates your brain and improves its condition, making it function better. To summon great memories, you can, for instance, go through an old album, looking through those ridiculous moments of childhood and youth, and you can also reminiscent about times you were deeply in love when the world seemed at its best. Whatever method you use to recall good times, the positive emotions generated are bound to do your brain a lot of good. Actually, the nice feeling is likely to make any challenges before you appear insignificant.

(7) Reduce intake of saturated fats

Do you know why it is necessary to cut down on saturated fats? And can you tell what fats are referred to as saturated fats? Firstly, the reason you need to cut down on saturated fats is that they are neither good for your heart, nor good for brain. These fats strain the heart while slowing down the brain function. In fact, there was a study done in Canada, specifically by staff from the University of Toronto, and its findings were that rats fed on 40% fatty diet weakened their mental function and marred their memory, and their general awareness actually deteriorated. This mess became even worse when the rats' diet had its saturated fats increased.

As for the fats that constitute saturated fats, they include fats from ordinary meat as well as those from dairy products. These end up forming the bad cholesterol, otherwise referred to as LDL, which then becomes an inconvenience to the flow of blood supplying oxygen to your brain.

What you actually need to do to remain in good health is to consume 30% calories from some form of fat, only ensuring that of that fat, the biggest proportion is from fish and seeds, and also nuts as well as olive oil. As much as possible, you are better off avoiding fats from snacks and fast foods because most of these have trans-fat, which end up raising your level of bad cholesterol.

Do you know why it is necessary to cut down on saturated fats? And can you tell what fats are referred to as saturated fats? Firstly, the reason you need to cut down on saturated fats is that they are neither good for your heart, nor good for brain. These fats strain the heart while slowing down the brain function. In fact, there was a study done in Canada, specifically by staff from the University of Toronto, and its findings were that rats fed on 40% fatty diet weakened their mental function and marred their memory, and their general awareness actually deteriorated. This mess became even worse when the rats' diet had its saturated fats increased.

(8) Solve puzzles

You can rejuvenate your brain by filling out crosswords, solving jigsaw puzzles and such other mind teasing activities. In fact, you do not have to do puzzles that are extremely challenging for them to help improve your brain function. Doing those you enjoy most is sufficient.

(9) Listen to your best music

On this front, do not expect anyone to prescribe the type of music for you. Some people say Mozart works for them, but this cannot be said to be the universal prescription. If you feel that listening to Country music arouses your brain and makes it feel alive, then go for the Kenny Rogers, Charlie Pride, Dolly Parton and the like. And if you want to go the Rod Stewart or Leon Haywood way, it is acceptable too. The point here is, whether listening to Celine Dion or rocking to Michael Jackson, what is going to get you into the groove is not important. Just pick what makes you tick and set your mind free to do its jig. It is healthy and makes you reason better.

(10) Modify your mode of exercising

Let's say you have taken to reading books for brain exercise. Are you going to read comics all the time? You may wish to add thrillers to your collection, or even adventure novels. If your liking is to play indoor games, it is a good idea that you don't stick to, say, drafts alone. You could decide to challenge your mind with scrabble, and probably even chess. When you push your brain, it serves as an even better exercise for it. Do not hesitate to push your brain until you feel it has reached its limit.

(11) Limit your alcohol intake

A little wine may be good for health, but for sure, drinking lots of alcohol is damaging to the brain cells. When 3,500 Japanese men were subjected to an alcohol intake related study, it was found that those among them who took only a single drink each day improved their cognitive function as their age advanced, while that positive development did not happen with those among the lot who refrained abstained completely. However, among those who drank, the ones who increased their daily alcohol intake to around four drinks and beyond had their brain health deteriorate.

Binge drinking is particularly dangerous, as it is responsible for killing very many brain cells, and it also deters the brain form forming new cells 30 days after the binge drinking session. In short, in moderation, alcohol is beneficial to your brain, but taken liberally, it can hurt. You need to particularly guard against alcoholism.

(12) Engage in play

Are you familiar with the saying, all work no play? Well, they say it makes you a dull person. This is not an empty cliché. It is actually true that when you regularly have leisure play sessions, like playing cards, tug of war, jumping rope, even playing the child related hide and seek, your brain gets rejuvenated – and your soul, obviously, feels good. On the overall, doing playing for fun and not necessarily for competition relieves you of stress, and it helps the brain function. It even makes you better at thinking strategically.

(13) Allow yourself some sleep after learning

Do you know something interesting about sleep? It does not only give you some nice rest that enables you to think clearly when you awake, it also helps you to retain information. For instance, when you gloss over some key points of a topic just before you sleep, or you actually read something important and soon you fall asleep, chances of you retaining that information correctly in your brain rises by between 20% and 30%.

Anyway, if you feel that reading just before bed mars your sleep when you finally fall asleep, write down your key point, if not what you have read in entirety, and then proceed to sleep. Your brain will relax and accept sleep and the information will be triggered to recall later when you read what you wrote down.

(14) Concentrate on what you are doing

Maintaining your focus when you are handling a task increases your brainpower. For that reason, you need to concentrate on whatever you are doing, avoiding distractions. You need to realize that whenever you choose something over another thing that was equally important to you, chances are you will be distracted during your chosen task. That means you cannot perform it as well because your brainpower will, most likely, not be at its optimum. Such thoughts of something pending lie just below your consciousness, and you may even try to deny that you are thinking about it because it is not exactly in your consciousness. Nevertheless, they mar your thinking and you cannot think as clearly as you otherwise could.

What you need to do is form a habit to find out if there is

something pending in your mind, something that is a potential distraction. Once you have identified it, deal with it before embarking on the important task at hand. If, for instance, it is a phone call you feel needs to be made, do it and put the thought to rest. This leaves you more relaxed, and you can, from then on, think clearly.

(15) Embrace love making

Should you embrace love making because it helps make your relationship better? Probably – well, yes. However, there is more to love making than making the bond with your partner stronger. It instigates physical contact between you and your partner, and such intimate physical contact is, especially for women, great for concentration. It also makes them feel emotionally much better than before.

Delving into some little biology, if, as a woman, you engage in regular physical contact, say once a week, your menstrual cycle becomes more fertile and regular, and you end up pushing forward your menopause as your estrogen levels rise. This whole process whose basis is intimate physical contact is said to delay the aging process and, of course, this means your brain will be working better for longer. In case you had no idea, decreased levels of estrogen in women happen to be associated with a fall in brain activity, as well as poor memory. As you have just read, regular physical contact is great for women in this regard, and when you consider the high probability of it leading to sex, it gets even better. This is because enjoying regular sex enhances brain activity and significantly improves your memory.

Something important you need to note under this point of using love making as a brain enhancing tool is that it does not matter if anyone gets an orgasm or not. The bonding bit that comes with physical intimacy is what counts in improving your brain function. In the same vein, sex need not be sex for the sake of it – it needs to be real love making; an act meant to make the parties happy and closer. That is why women are discouraged from unnecessarily withholding sex from their partners, because it is bound to hurt them as well, denying themselves a dose of natural brain medication.

(16) Put passion into your activities

Can you visualize yourself doing something that you love? Now move a notch higher and visualize yourself doing something that draws crazy passion from you? When you are excited about something you love and you do it with passion, needless to say, the results are normally excellent. It may even be a tough task, but if you are passionate about it, you get an adrenaline rush just by thinking about the chance to do it. Incidentally, these are the kinds of tasks that also instigate the production of the so-called happy hormones, those that keep your brain healthy and active in a big way.

Chapter 7: How to Sharpen Your Skills in Decision Making

Do you think you can sharpen your skills in decision making by doing what you always do? That is your comfort zone and if you fear to venture out of it, it means your skills will remain unchanged. Yet the more new challenges arise, the more the need to improve the skills you already have, so as to be able to cope with those emerging challenges. One important thing you cannot ignore is that every time you get your brain learning something new, you end up stimulating it, and that positive impact makes the brainwork like a well-lubricated machine. Finally, but very important, let us just say your ability and competence in decision making is very important, because it is on the basis of your decisions that action is taken. Of course, whenever you make a good decision, progress is great, and the converse is true.

Unique Techniques of Honing Decision Making Skills

Engage in art or culture based activities

The idea here is to get involved in activities that are related to art or culture, because those are areas that encourage you to be creative. Of course, as you have already seen, creativity is associated with an improved brain function. Practically speaking, what you need to do is set aside three separate hours in a week, and during every one of those one-hour sessions, you do a task that calls for you to be creative. Normally, it is a good idea to choose something that is new to you, because then you will not just be exercising your creativity, you will also be challenging your brain. Those two – being creative and challenging your brain – provide a good exercise for your brain and at the end of the day you have a brain that is great at decision-making.

Some of the best activities to learn include playing the guitar, painting, building house models or a train track model and so on. Once you spend time expanding your horizons, the result is a boost to your brain activity, and improved decision making skills.

Learn new language skills

Are you English? What do you think if you were to learn, say, German, or French? One thing is for sure is that acquiring the right language skills is bound to be a challenge for starters. Although ultimately you could end up being good at the newly acquired foreign language, it will have taken you great effort in trying to remember pronunciations, gender for those languages whose lexicons have gender classifications, and so on. Understandably, therefore, you will end up sharpening your memory, and the vigorous exercise you will have given your brain will end up improving your skills in decision-making.

Incorporate people of varying ages in your social circle

As far as you can tell, which age group knows best in every issue that comes up? You may be tempted to say the older generation is wiser than the young generation and so they know best, but how about that part that relates to every issue? How much good advice can they offer you on matters of technology, for example?

The point here is that no single person has the monopoly of knowledge, and because you want to remain knowledgeable so that you are resourceful as a decision maker, it is important that you relate with people of all ages. From people older than yourself, you could tap into their experience, learn the need for patience, and so on. From the young, you could learn to let loose once in a while so that you can relax, and this is good for your brain because as you relax and have some fun you also give your brain time to rejuvenate.

Engage in regular physical exercise

You may wonder if the reason for this is to tone your body, and while toning your body makes you look nice and hence boosts your self-confidence, this is not the sole reason. Think of the many people you meet and socialize with, some of them entirely new to you there before, making you a happy person. You have already seen in earlier chapters that happiness makes you a better decision maker, and here you have that happiness, plus the improvement of your brain function courtesy of a healthy body.

Perform experiments in cookery

It helps to improve your ability in decision making when you learn how to cook and if you already know how to cook, how to prepare new recipes. You need to realize that there is a good deal of decision making in cookery, as you must think of the best combination of ingredients, the different options you have as far as heat level is concerned, and so on. So, cookery can give you good practice in decision-making.

Build an online social community
The idea here is to build a community of online pals with whom you can discuss ideas and experiences, and even organize going on short trips together, have picnics and even attend other events.

Weigh advantages against disadvantages
Your decision making process cannot be complete without you singling out the advantages, and also pointing out the disadvantages, of the decision you are about to take. After knowing what comprises the positives and what comprises the negatives, you then need to compare them, and if you find the disadvantages outweighing the advantages, you may wish to go check out another option that you may have ignored.

In decision-making, it is fine to consult other people you deem resourceful, but you need to realize the buck stops with you. So, even if you listen to advice from other people, adopt it as yours after due consideration. Essentially, therefore, whatever decision you make, let it be one you can own up to; one you personally believe is the best option.

How to Ensure Your Decisions Are Foolproof

You have just gone through the techniques to use in

improving your skills in decision-making. Now you are going to learn how to ensure you do not present questionable decisions, but well refined decisions that have been subjected to scrutiny. For sure, you do not want to base your work on a decision you made only for things to go bad. On the contrary, you want the decision you make to be the basis of success as far as your project is concerned. Even if something were to go wrong after executing your decision, you need to be able to minimize the damage.

Techniques to Help Refine Your Decisions

Do a cost-benefit analysis

Ask yourself how much is it going to cost to implement this decision, and what are the benefits that are likely to accrue from this decision if it is implemented? There is no harm either in comparing such costs and benefits with the next best option, and probably a few more options, so that you will be able to tell for sure what your opportunity costs will have been. In short, in taking this decision and not the one you consider the next best, what will you be sacrificing? Is it worth sacrificing? If you weigh such matters, you will be certain that the decision you have taken is the best choice for the situation under consideration.

Trim down your options

Conducting a final analysis of several possible decisions can be exhausting and time consuming. If there is a monetary cost involved in doing the cost-benefit analysis, it means you would have to incur relatively high costs if you were to compare all those options. For that matter, you need to narrow down your options to just a few, so that you do not incur too much cost and also so as not to overwhelm yourself. At the same time, it can be confusing to compare a long list of options, which is not good for decision-making.

Check the degree of significance

Do you know how detailed accountants are? Well, they really are, and if you watch them calculate your personal costs, you might see them determine how much you spend per hour, even when you have not left the house. Nevertheless, detailed as they are, they do leave an allowance for insignificant figures, that even if disagreeable, they can live with. This is the same reasoning you need to use here. When you look at the decision you are trying to make, is it very important when fitted into the bigger picture? If so, then, by all means, take all the time you have to. However, if it is one of those decisions that cannot make much impact whether you make the best the best possible or you do it shoddily, then that is not worth spending a lot of time on.

If you go by this principle of significance, you will have ample time to dedicate to sensitive decisions, as well as those that can have a drastic impact on the project at hand. Actually, what experts do advise is that you assess the significance of the decision you are trying to make and then give yourself strict timelines, so that you have a definite deadline beyond which you are not going to deal with that decision again.

Avoid worrying about petty stuff

The point is, if you begin worrying about how many fun programs you will have missed by the time you get home from work, when will you have time to think about the number of clients you will manage to contact within a given period of time? Sweating the small stuff is unnecessarily tiring and time consuming and it kind of steals the time for more serious stuff, which can actually make an impact in your life.

Conduct sufficient research

Is this something we always do? Unfortunately, although on paper this is a must-do and almost everyone knows its importance, sometimes you may get excited about an opportunity and rush to make a decision without sufficient information. Often such decisions prove to be expensive as you get to discover some downside only after you have already committed yourself or the contract is underway. Therefore, in order to avoid disappointment, make your decision only after doing due diligence, which in reality comprises proper research.

Seek informed views

Who actually has the monopoly of information and knowledge? If you accept you do not have it, why then would you hesitate to seek the views of someone you consider knowledgeable? And mind you in this case we are not talking of people who can only feed you with myths. Rather, we are talking of people who are well informed in the field under review. In fact, you could even consult people who are not necessarily experts in the field, but if, in your opinion, they are mature people who have the capacity to weigh issues in an objective manner, you would be fine seeking their views. Even seeking the opinion of certain people who may have had experiences that are similar to the one you are facing is a good idea. Entrepreneurs employ the right people to do the work they are expert at and do not hesitate in consulting them.

Chapter 8: Using Questioning in Critical Thinking

Why do you normally ask questions? Obviously there are things you want to know and understand with more clarity. Even those questions that you sometimes ask just because you are curious are good. Do you not feel more enlightened after someone has answered your question? You may have satisfied your curiosity now, if that is all you were interested in, but sometime later, the information you achieved knowing about out of curiosity becomes handy.

Incidentally, you do not have to ask questions exclusively to other people. You can also pose questions to yourself. For one, directing questions to yourself is one way of exercising your brain, and this, as you have already seen, is great for critical thinking.

General Benefits of Asking Questions

Any time you ask a question:

- You clear any vagueness that may have existed

- You clear any possible confusion

- You automatically find yourself streamlining your thinking

Any time you are considering asking questions in the context of critical thinking, you cannot fail to notice their positive contribution in setting that time's agenda. As you would expect, the response somebody gives you when you ask a question is relevant to the particular situation that you are dealing with. Your questions actually provide direction to your thinking. In order to invoke critical thinking, it is important that you design your questions in a certain way.

How to Design Questions to Enhance Critical Thinking

- Create questions that help to build your body of knowledge

- Create questions that help you improve your understanding of the given situation

- Create questions help you in analyzing the data and facts at your disposal.

- Design your questions in such a way as to help you synthesize the information that you have.

So, now you know the kind of questions you are supposed to create. The big question is how do you accomplish this? Simple! There are some dos and don'ts that you can adhere to, and following them will help you in creating the most helpful questions.

Dos and Don'ts in Creating Questions

Ensure the questions you create are not one dimensional

Any idea what one-dimensional questions are? Well, they are those questions that call for a single word answer, either yes or no. Does such a question really provoke anyone's mind to think in a critical way? Surely, it cannot.

Plan your questions in advance

You may wonder what the timing has got to do with critical thinking but, if you pause to consider it, someone making up questions as the questioning session proceeds is unlikely to have helpful questions. The kind of planning referred to in this regard involves preparing your questions early enough, so that you do not end up designing questions in a hurry.

Do you know who brought up this issue of serious questioning in the context of critical thinking? It was an educator called Benjamin Bloom, and the style of questioning he proposed was adopted in the name of *The Bloom Taxonomy*. There are specific meanings you need to understand in the context of The Bloom Taxonomy, particularly the meaning of Knowledge, of comprehension and also of analysis of issues.

- In this context, knowledge stands for the facts, and you know facts are things you can remember. It also includes any opinions you may hold, and also the ideas you currently have.

- As for comprehension, it is your ability to interpret the information you have in some form of language that you understand well.

- When you speak of synthesizing knowledge and also putting it to use, it means your ability to interpret the information that is in your possession, and then utilizing it in situations that are entirely new.

Generally speaking, you can consider questioning as that critical thinking tool that puts you in a much better position than before; to understand other situations that are similar to that which you have managed to evaluate during your session of critical thinking.

How to Design Appropriate Questions for Critical Thinking

1. Ask questions that court knowledge

You are capable of asking anything you want, aren't you? Yet not everything you ask will earn you a response that is helpful to your critical thinking process. If you want to design questions that will get you responses useful to critical thinking, you need to first of all be sure what you are interested in achieving using the information you get. Do you know how to establish where your interest lies as far as accomplishing a goal is concerned? In order to establish where you are heading with your critical thinking:

- Review The Much You Know About The Situation Under Scrutiny

- Make An Effort Of Remembering The Facts Of The Situation, And The Terminologies Relevant In Analyzing And Understanding The Situation

- List All The Ideas You Know, Which You Deem Relevant

- Note All The Answers You May Already Have Regarding The Queries You Have Been Having.

After doing these, sort of, preliminaries, you will realize what you will be gathering thereafter is stuff that is relevant to the situation, and very helpful in your critical thinking process. In short, you will not be risking collecting double or duplicate information, or stuff that is of no consequence to the process. Now that you are set to design the questions to use in your critical thinking process, do you know how you ought to frame them so that you can court the best answers?

How to Design Questions to Attract Informative Response

- What do you call this thing or that one?

- In which category does this thing or that one belong?

- Why do you get this response or that reaction after doing this or that?

- How can this or that other occurrence be explained?

- When are the times when this phenomenon or that other phenomenon surface?

Create questions that enable comprehension

It is important that you appreciate the context within which the information you have received has been supplied, so that you are able to do your critical thinking in an effective way. It is also important that you are able to put all the information together for analysis, so that the information can serve your purpose well. When you get down to it, what you intend to accomplish by your comprehension questions include:

- Organizing ideas, as well as facts that are in your possession, with a view to comparing them

- Translating and also interpreting those ideas and facts in a way that they convey something meaningful

- Giving suitable descriptions to the ideas and facts that you have

- Identifying all ideas that you find are of primary importance, and then you organize and arrange them in what you consider your order of priority.

Do you know the next step you need to take, now that you have finished establishing what you want to achieve or accomplish? Well, it is time to formulate the questions you want to use.

How Best to Tailor Comprehension Questions

- How do you imagine this one idea readily compares with that other idea; or how do some two ideas contrast against each other?

- What possible explanation can you provide for this particular appearance or that other different appearance?

- What are the facts, according to you, that support your position?

- What, really, is the possible evidence that makes you hold the position that you do?

Build questions that help with the actual application of knowledge

Do you, incidentally, know why questions happen to be important in knowledge usage? The reason is that while you may have a lot of knowledge, as long as you do not understand how best to utilize it, the problem you have been facing will still persist. What you are lacking is the most appropriate technique, which you can employ to have the knowledge you have work for you. It is for this reason that you are required to ask questions that are relevant to the use of the information you have.

Examples regarding how to design questions:

- What possible examples do you think you can give to be solutions for this or that or even that other challenge?

- How do you think you can show that you are comfortable and conversant with this or that?

- In your personal view, what would you say is the best approach whenever you are trying to handle this or even that?

- What, in your thinking, would happen, just supposing things were to turn out one way or the other?

Design questions that are likely to enhance analysis
What is within your reach to help in critical analysis? Well, you have the mass of knowledge you gathered, and from that you are going to derive the information you need. Of course, the information you intend to use in critical thinking must have enough credible material to support it. How precisely can you determine which particular material to use in your critical analysis? Remember what you have right now is general information. To be sure about the specific material to use, you need to first break down that mass of information in your possession.

What You Achieve by Breaking down Your General Information
- You are able to identify the motives of the various ideas contained therein, and all else that is involved

- You are able to single out the causes that are entrenched within the massive information that you have

- You will be able to single out inferences

- You will be in a position to identify evidence within that information that you have in your possession

At the time of analyzing information in regard to critical analysis, the way to frame questions is as follows:

- What possible inference do you make at the time of weighing you weigh the different pieces of information?

- What place would you put pieces of information in your possession?

- How can you classify this, that or that other idea?

- When you identify a single concept, would you be in a position to distinguish the actual parts that form it?

Create queries that seek to evaluate

Do you know what you are trying to achieve here? It is to validate the opinion that you will have developed by virtue of the very information you have, and also on the basis of the very technique you have used in the application of that information. This is the stage you are supposed to be passing judgment on what you have observed, and also on what you have experienced during the whole process of critical thinking.

How you can frame evaluation questions:

- How, in your view, should you contrast this particular idea against that other idea?

- Which one of the two, or even more items, do you take to be the best, under these particular circumstances?

- How, do you imagine, you can rate this person's performance against some performance of another person?

- What have you possibly established to be the essence of engaging this particular resource or that other one?

- If someone happened to ask you what you would have preferred earlier, what would you have volunteered as your suggestion

Design questions that are specifically geared towards aiding in synthesis

What you want to do at this very stage is to try and synthesize all that you have personally observed and done, and then you proceed to develop some solution that is unique to your specific issue. Of course, by now you will have visualized what the general direction is that you intend to go with your decision, and that is after you have consolidated the entire information in your possession. It is also after you have analyzed that information. However, at this juncture, it is important that you be specific regarding the cause of action you plan to take next.

How to design synthesis related queries:

- What do you really think about this specific idea or even that other idea?

- Do you, in any way, envisage having some alternative interpretation of this particular situation?

- Can you, by some chance, envisage a situation where can be another possibility, whereby you can get around this hurdle or that some other one?

Chapter 9: Critical Thinking Strategies

When do you consider doing critical thinking? The thing is, you are doing critical thinking all the time, sometimes knowingly and sometimes unknowingly. Mostly you get to do it unknowingly when you have gotten used to consciously engaging in critical thinking. So, if whenever there is an issue to be resolved you do not dash to conclusions but instead engage in critical thinking, even when you come across a light challenge on a casual basis, you are likely to find yourself analyzing it and evaluating it, before making any conclusions about it –is basically a positive thing.

Critical thinking is actually a very progressive way of learning, and you can see how this is when you consider what is involved. Consider you have the task to consolidate information, to organize it, to do an in-depth analysis of the body of information that you have, and ultimately, to synthesize that information. In fact, it does not count if finally you come up with a solution to the problem at hand. The fact that you have been able to find the relevant information, and you have critically processed it, means you have become a more informed person, a more enlightened one, than before you began trying to tackle the challenge. In short, even when you do not formally have some problem to solve, it is a good idea to practice critical thinking.

Funnily enough, some people take thinking to be an automated process, something that you just get into without a strategy. Well, you surely could go that way, thinking without putting much weight to what you are thinking, but if you get used to this, your mind is likely to come up with dull ideas, and not ideas that use creativity in a constructive way. Ultimately, you can become someone from whom people around you cannot expect much help in terms of ideas and problem solving skills. Why would you not want to be a resourceful person, which is what critical thinking makes you, when you surely have the potential? It doesn't make sense.

Let us now assume you are prepared to polish your skills in critical thinking. What should you be prepared to do? The answer, at this juncture, cannot be difficult, especially considering the much you have learnt in earlier chapters about the critical thinking process. Essentially, you want your performance in whatever task you engage in to be above average. So, it is up to you to take the process of critical thinking serious. Can you put it off until tomorrow? You need to take learning as a continuous process, because you want to be informed at all times; or at least most times. You also want to have mastery of critical thinking techniques, and also to be consistent in making use of them. You cannot afford to be a critical thinker today and not worry about it tomorrow. What will pleasantly surprise you is that once you have entered the shoes of a critical thinker, you are bound to experience positive change in your life, and particularly where your very personal development is concerned. Critical thinkers use their powers of deduction all the time.

So, can you now see you need to be adept at critical thinking if you are to be a great problem solver? If so, then you cannot afford to take critical thinking strategies lightly.

Key Strategies to Make You Great At Critical Thinking

Keep your focus on the challenge
Have you realized some people hardly want to spare their precious time giving attention to a problem at hand? What you will notice when you spare sufficient time to think about how to handle a particular challenge, you are able to adopt the right perspective to the issue, and also to assess the challenge comprehensively. You are often also able to consider the challenge within the circumstances that exist.

Of course, it is highly unlikely that you will always manage to come up with solutions for all the problems you try to solve, and that is true even when you come to a problem that is familiar or is similar to another one you handled in the past. The reason that makes every challenge different is that the environments within which different problems come up usually vary. The timing also matters for every challenge that you are faced with. Everything considered, you realize it pays to give special attention to every single challenge as it stands.

Practice asking critical questions
When do you think you would receive the best answer to a question? Would it be when you ask a general question, or when you ask a specific question? And when would you expect to receive a serious and helpful answer? Would it be

when you ask a question in a serious manner, or when you ask it in a casual manner? If you want to receive the most helpful answer to a question, the manner of asking matters a great deal. It is important that you tailor your questions in a way that is bound to provoke the person you are addressing into giving you relevant answers that are also helpful. Also when you are trying to design questions that will help you during the time of doing research, it is important that you frame those questions in a manner that will lead them to sources relevant to the issue at hand. You are also able to locate relevant material faster.

Get verifiable evidence
It is recommended that you get into the habit of learning and supporting your ideas by way of evidence that is verifiable, and also by way of logical thinking.

Do proper analysis
It is also a great idea for you to get used to analyzing whatever issue you have before you attempt to make any deductions. Something else you need to do in the same vein is proper reasoning and also proper evaluation of situations and challenges.

Do reasonable interpretation
It is important that you learn to interpret issues at length and in depth, as you avoid the urge to embrace information solely at face value.

Synthesize ideas
It is a good idea that you practice synthesizing the ideas at your disposal.

Break down complex questions

You need to learn to handle questions that are complex by first of all breaking them down into smaller and more manageable ones.

Learn to make decisions

You need to learn the art of decision making, so you can succeed in decision making once you have evaluated the possible outcomes.

Learn to generate and evaluate options

Learn too the art of generating options, and practice evaluating those options before you proceed to select the most appropriate one for your situation.

Be detail oriented

Practice paying attention to detail because that is how you will derive sound meanings that are as close as possible to precision.

Think high level

Get used to thinking at a high level so that you are able to analyze challenges that you face in real life, and also to solve them.

Get used to day-to-day critical thinking

It is best that you get used to critical thinking even on the simple problems that you encounter on a day-to-day basis. Once you do this, applying critical thinking to serious challenges is likely to come relatively easy thereafter.

Categorize your ideas always

It is good practice, and a helpful one too, to categorize the ideas you have as per the value you attach to each one of them.

Reflect
When you do your thinking, try and be consciously reflective.

Focus on solving the problem
Learn to focus on tasks that are geared towards solving the problem at hand, while refraining from doing tasks that would be termed redundant.

Make an effort of learning
Be someone who is open to fresh ideas, and try not to stick stubbornly to old ideas. In the same vein, you need to be prepared to look at issues from varying perspectives.

Find more suitable solutions
You need to be seeking better solutions at all times, instead of being complacent with old solutions.

Embrace alternatives
You need to be open to receiving other solutions you may not have dealt with before.

Embrace fresh techniques, solutions as well as ideas
It is advisable that you respect the ideas other people offer, and also the different points of view they present to you. Surround yourself with talented people.

Confirm information veracity
You need to always check the veracity of any information you intend to use, even when you have gotten that information from published books or from the Internet. Even if you are picking information from things you or other people have observed, just check it out for accuracy and credibility. Let us

just, in fact, say you need to check the veracity of all information you are considering for use at all times. This helps you to have more accurate information at hand.

Assess repercussions
Before you embark on solving a problem, make a point of evaluating any repercussions that are likely to arise.

Be prepared for collaboration
It is a good idea to be open to collaboration between you and other resourceful people in matters of problem solving.

Keep to basic intellectual standards
Ensure you observe the basic intellectual standards at the time of dealing with challenges of varying kinds.

Here, the standards being referred to happen to be of a universal nature, and they include clarity, accuracy and precision, relevance and the idea of analyzing issues with breadth as well as depth. These standards also include logic, and the ability to assess significance as far as information and other factors are concerned.

Chapter 10: The Need to Think Logically

Is there anyone who cannot benefit from logical thinking? Remember, by logical thinking we mean you having a reason for whatever conclusion you arrive at in a case, and being able to predict what is bound to happen if you do certain things with the input of valid facts. Logical thinking is something you do devoid of emotion, and which is not influenced by the urge to romanticize. If you are going to come up with solid solutions based on the reality represented by facts, then surely everyone who takes the route of logic can benefit.

In fact, when it comes to the benefits of logical thinking, it does not count that you are in this or that department and not in any other. Logical thinking is beneficial regardless of your department. One thing you should be happy about is that it is possible for you to sharpen your logical thinking and once you do that, you will be able to make worthwhile decisions later on in life.

How to Improve and Enhance Logical Thinking

Making use of a condition statement
In this process of enhancing logical thinking, you need to begin by creating a condition statement. Condition statements are those that say if you do this, something of that sort will happen, or if you fail to do this, something of that nature will happen. In short, what you allege will happen is dependent on the occurrence or non-occurrence of something else. In our case, there needs to be a problem or a challenge under consideration for you to be called upon to make a decision.

A good example of a condition statement is when you are warning a student about the potential of suspension from school. You can say something like:

If you destroy school property you will be suspended.

Something is going to happen. What? You, the student, are going to be suspended.
On what condition is the student going to be suspended? The student is going to be suspended on condition he or she destroys school property.

You can term what we have just alleged as either a *logic statement* or *condition statement*. The last bit of that statement is the ultimate result of the condition coming to pass. Whenever the condition becomes a reality, the anticipated result also materializes, becoming reality as well. People who like doing mathematics, and particularly, calculus, often get to use condition statement.

Making proper use of the premise as well as the conclusion

We are still looking at the condition statement, and saying you need to understand in depth how this statement operates. Within that condition statement is what you can term the premise, and there is also what you can term the conclusion shorthand. In essence, both of them are terms as far as logic is concerned. The term that comes first is the premise that you hold. The second part of the statement is the conclusion. When you are dealing with a condition statement, the conclusion becomes true only when the premise proves to be true.

Why would anyone be so keen on discussing the terms in a condition statement? The reason is that such statements bear facts that are the basis of further analysis when we are dealing with logic. It is your understanding of the very first condition statement that will help you understand three other major components that are borne by the statement. Those components are what is termed, converse, then the inverse and also the contra-positive. You need to understand these three components very well so that you are able to avoid reasoning that is faulty, and also so that you are able to detect it any time, someone else is trying to apply it.

Using the converse statement

For now, we want to take a situation where the premise is equal to 'x', and the conclusion is 'y'. We can proceed to say that 'y' is, conversely, equal to 'x'. What we are basically saying is that if 'x' is equal to 'y', you can make a converse statement that 'y' is equal to 'x'. The converse statement is the way it is, by virtue of the first statement holding true.

Essentially, therefore, what you take as the converse is, kind of, the reverse of your premise, and it is also your conclusion.

In the example we gave earlier of the student being suspended, you could create the converse and say, if you were suspended, then it was because you destroyed school property. However, you may already have noted that the converse may not be necessarily true because, like in the example you are using, the student could have been suspended because of other mistakes and not necessarily destroying school property. Making an assumption that the converse will hold true can lead to what is termed *fallacy of false syllogism*, something like:

- If a student destroys school property, he or she is suspended

- The student has destroyed property

- The student has been suspended

Using the inverse statement

When you speak of the inverse, you are referring to the original statement that you keep unaltered. That way, the premise plus the conclusion remain unchanged. The only difference here is that the two happen to negate each other.

The inverse of the example we used of the student and being suspended would go something like this:

If you do not destroy school property, you will not be suspended

There are those times when the inverse happens to be true, but this case of the student and possible suspension, is one such case. There are also those cases where the inverse happens not to be true. Here is an example of a statement whose inverse is untrue:

Premise and conclusion: *If you drop the camera in water, it will be destroyed*

The inverse: *If you do not drop the camera in water, it will not be destroyed*

Now, does it mean the camera cannot be destroyed any other way? It, obviously, can. So, the inverse in this second example happens to be untrue. As you can see, you need to be careful how you use inverse reasoning.

Using the contra-positive statement

This contra-positive statement has two sides to it. There is the converse of what you find as the inverse, and there is the inverse of what you consider the converse. Is this confusing? Well, it is not exactly difficult. It actually encompasses a negation of the premise as well as the conclusion, as well as a reversal. The contra-positive of the student statement would be:

If you do not destroy school property, you will not be suspended

If you assume the truth of the very original statement or that conditional statement, that contra-positive happens to be the only alternative that is going to be consistently true.

Using necessary Conditions

This statement of necessary conditions happens to be related to the conditional statement and other related statements. It bears ideas of necessary conditions, or of sufficient conditions.

Now, what would you say a necessary condition is? Well, it is a condition that has to be fulfilled, in order for some anticipated outcome to succeed. For instance, for the student not to be suspended, he or she must not destroy school property. As such, avoiding destruction of school property is necessary if you are to prevent the student's suspension.

Using Sufficient Conditions

What you term sufficient condition in the example of student is alleging that destroying school property is sufficient to get the student suspended. It guarantees in no uncertain terms that a certain result is going to occur, and that result is dependent on that condition provided.

Using Necessary but Not Sufficient

You can sometimes have necessary conditions that are, nevertheless, not sufficient. Avoiding destruction of school property is necessary if you are to prevent the student from being suspended. However, even if you managed to do that, the student could still be suspended for other misdemeanors. For example, the same student might sneak away from school or become rude to a teacher, and get suspended for it. As such, whereas avoiding destruction of school property is necessary, it is not sufficient to keep the student from suspension.

Using Sufficient yet Not Necessary

You can have a condition that is sufficient, but it is not necessary. Suppose a student were to destroy school property under duress. Would that make the school administration suspend that student? Very likely it would not. In short, damaging school property would ordinarily be sufficient to get the student suspended, but it happens not to be always a necessary condition for expulsion.

Using Not Necessary or Sufficient

Sometimes, you can have conditions that are not necessary, and other times conditions that are not sufficient, in relation to the result. In order to avoid being suspended from school, it is neither necessary nor sufficient for the student to destroy school property. If you master working with these conditions and when they can apply and not apply, when they are sufficient to make given results happen or not happen, and so on, will you not be working as logically as a computer?

Chapter 11: The Make-Up of a Skilled Critical Thinker

Do you know what makes up a great critical thinker? Obviously, such a person would need to be able to do all that appertains to a critical thinker, as explained in earlier chapters of this book. As a simple guide, you can read the attributes as well as abilities that you need to possess or develop, for you to qualify as a great critical thinker.

Attributes of Great Critical Thinkers

They have tolerance
In critical thinking, you need to delight at hearing varying views, as you enjoy a vibrant debate and are an active listener.

They have analytical skills
Critical thinkers, of necessity, must have analytical skills, and if you do not have them you need to develop them. You are not expected to be one of those people who accept

whatever has been said without thinking or taking a minute to analyze it. Critical thinkers prefer to construct arguments properly, and also to come up with sound reasons, before they can make any conclusions. Once you have analyzed the problem well, the conclusions you draw are bound to be sound.

They have confidence

What is it you can really accomplish without an iota of confidence? People would actually shove everything – baked and half-baked – down your throat. So, in order not to find yourself in a position where you do other people's bidding without thinking about its validity and worth, you need to have, at least, some level of confidence. This way, you will be able to evaluate the different views given, and then determine if such views would contribute positively to solving the problem that you are facing. The need for confidence is absolutely necessary particularly when the views you want to review are from people senior to you, or people whom you greatly respect.

They express curiosity

Critical thinkers are curious people. After all, how are you going to learn if you are not eager to know what is happening? Curiosity, in the context of critical thinking, is a basic ingredient in the acquisition and development of ideas as well as insights.

They seek the truth

You can only be a great critical thinker if you seek to establish the truth and validity of information before drawing your conclusions. In fact, critical thinkers who are worth their salt do not worry that once they establish what the truth is, it might end up negating the premise they earlier held. Instead, they are prepared to replace their earlier convictions, if they happen to be unfounded, with the objective truth. In doing this, critical thinkers do not work for their own interest but for the common good.

How to Assess the Worthiness of Views

In the process of critical thinking, you need to check what it would take to make each view worthwhile. In the process, you need to extract evidence that you can establish from tested theories that you consider worth consideration. What you will effectively be doing is referred to as the Assertibility Question, or the AQ. Here, you will be, presumably, seeking to find out what actual evidence qualifies you to assert confidently that the claim under consideration is true. This form of verification is what distinguishes information worth using from that which is not helpful in your circumstances.

How to test your theories scientifically:

- Does the idea you are weighing tally with common sense or is it a crazy idea?

- Who came up with the idea? Is it someone with some obvious bias that leans towards wishing the idea to be true?

- Did the person proposing the idea make use of statistics in a manner that can be termed honest? Have they backed up the idea with credible references, or with other credible work that backs up the idea?

- Is the idea you are considering one that has too much information to be believed, or too little to be of significant use?

- Are those people proposing the idea open about the idea, its source, how they got the idea, and so on?

- Are there factors that may restrict you from employing the idea under scrutiny?

Understanding Cycles of Consciousness

How consistent do you imagine your level of consciousness is? It actually fluctuates, increasing and decreasing at different times of the day. Often, you will find your consciousness going through a 90 min. cycle and within it is a 30 min cycle where your level of consciousness happens to be lower. This low cycle is the one you need to learn to identify, so that you can monitor your mental state well. Can you tell why it is important to monitor the state of your mind? Well, once you have become good at monitoring when your consciousness is up and when it is down, you are able to select the timing for serious thinking, or the time most appropriate to deal with issues of significance. This is because you can tell when your mind is awake and when it is semi-awake. You will know instinctively when you can make solid decisions and what time of day is your best.

The Need to Learn Some New Skill

Have you noticed that a good number of people appear to be forgetful as they advance in age? Why not take advantage of your brain while it is still healthy and working in a youthful way to learn fresh skills? In the process of learning such skills, you end up making your brain stronger and better placed to think logically for many more years. In fact, you do not have to do a complex exercise. A simple task such as learning a word you did not know is sufficient to improve your brain function. There happens to be a close correlation between your working vocabulary and your intelligence. One thing you need to know is once you have a wide variety of vocabulary to use, and especially new ones, you get to learn fresh ways as well as nuances to link up ideas. In short, by putting your good mind to use, you get to re-energize the brain, keeping it young.

Learning To Write For Reading

Do you know how interesting writing can be? If you consider writing for other people to read, whether it is an article you want published or a book you intend to write for public consumption, it becomes even more interesting. As you think up ways to keep your readers captivated, you unleash your creativeness and stimulate your mind, and as you may already be aware, stimulating your mind keeps it youthful.

Going Through Aromatherapy

Here you are looking at the use of nicely scented essential oils for aromatherapy. It relaxes you when you are exhausted and makes your mind alert after an elongated dull period. Luckily, you need just a couple of drops of some nice, relaxing essential oil, to make you feel vibrant and motivated. Some great essential oils you could use include lemon essential oil, cypress, peppermint, and even orange. The easiest way of doing such aromatherapy is applying a couple of drops of your selected essential oil onto some cotton ball, and then inhaling the oil scent.

Taking User Friendly Drugs

Have you heard of students doing whatever they can to remain alert during the exam season? This book is going to cite some brands of herbal tea, such as gingko Biloba and Gotu kola, which give you a boost whenever you feel like having a sharp, alert mind. These herbal teas are known to be healthy because they increase blood flow into your brain in a natural way, thus enhancing your concentration.

Keeping Your Brain Active and Busy

Do you think it is a good idea to build your brainpower? If you are actually going to succeed in enhancing your brainpower, you need to embrace the resourcefulness of people around you. It is inspiring and also stimulating. Something else you can do is read magazines and other reading material. It is a good idea to have discussions not just with different people, but also about different places, including new places. Such discussions help you to identify and utilize new opportunities. It is important to note that, irrespective of your occupation or your age, it is important to challenge your brain and to do that consistently, so that it is always operating at its most efficient. Luckily, you do not need to engage in something complicated. Reading Shakespeare and playing a game of chess is as good as acquiring a fresh skill. The idea is to protect your brain from getting rusty by keeping it busy.

Chapter 12: How to Develop 5 Critical Thinking Types

Do you remember the mention that critical thinking encompasses different stages? And all those stages are tackled by leaders who think strategically; people who are able to appreciate the prevailing state of affairs and the possibilities that lie ahead. Such leaders operate from a long-term perspective that also happens to be broad. In short, great thinkers do not base their decision making on a short-term perspective. Instead, they collect relevant information, and then they make their decisions in a very timely manner.

At the same time, such strategic leaders endeavor to strike a good balance between what they visualize for the future, and what they know to be the day-to-day reality of life. They are capable of peeping into the future, to get a picture of where the organization needs to be at a given future date, and seeing vividly what the consequences of their decisions are likely to be. Impressively, these leaders do this without losing track of the things that go on in the present time.

Any idea how many modes of thinking strategic leaders make

use of? They are actually five. You will prove to be a leading strategic leader depending on how much you are able to utilize each mode of thinking, and how appropriate the timing is for that particular mode of thinking.

Critical Thinker's Modes of Thinking

The critical thinking mode
There is the critical thinking mode that happens to be the mental process of analyzing situations in an objective manner, and which encompasses collection of information from every credible source possible, evaluation of aspects that are tangible and those that are intangible. This mode also includes considering the implications of whatever action you decide to take.

The mode of implementation thinking
This mode happens to be the ability to get your ideas as well as plans together in an organized way. These ideas and plans work effectively well.

The mode of conceptual thinking
This is the mode of thinking that uses your ability to establish connections or even patterns between ideas that are abstract and those that make a real picture.

The mode of innovative thinking
This mode entails generating fresh ideas, or getting fresh ways of approaching issues, to enable you generate possibilities and possible opportunities.

The mode of intuitive thinking

This mode encompasses your ability to perceive something to be true, doing it without prior knowledge about the facts involved, and factoring it in a suitable way into the ultimate decision.

For many years, many leaders got away with basic critical thinking as well as implementation thinking. However, many leaders today know different. This is a superfast world, and it has become important to conceptualize and innovate, as well as also doing intuitive thinking, particularly in the environment of industries.

As for leaders in the business sector, there is still need to collect and analyze information, come up with decisions, and to then implement those decisions well. However, these days, leaders now take massive data, and that data now comes from a wide range of sources. They do their analysis and make decisions with full knowledge that any moment the data in their possession could change. For those who have the ability to think over possibilities, observe patterns as well as connections that are not obvious to other people, they, definitely, have a big competitive advantage. These people are able to see the data with fresh eyes, so to speak.

Have you realized some people are naturally highly intuitive? They actually are, yet many are the people who do not have the natural gift of intuition. Nevertheless, basic leadership skills that are helpful in critical thinking need to be developed and enhanced.

How to Develop Fundamental Leadership Skills

Always check around

You need to always check around, browsing business websites and reading relevant publications, so you can learn the way other successful organizations implement their strategies, to be able to raise their great competitive advantage.

Be free to shift directions

It is a great idea to adjust the directions you had initially set, in order to pursue fresh goals whenever strategic opportunities emerge. You need to ponder over what it is that is making you remain on the path you are on, and to push yourself to consider whether you should, or should not, alter your plans. Every time you are doing this, it is best that you focus on the worst-case scenario.

Do not follow short-cuts

Whenever there is a problem to be solved, it is recommended that you avoid going for a quick fix. Instead, you need to take your time looking at the problem at hand, taking your time analyzing possible solutions, and finally creating a checklist that will help you trigger your thoughts towards consequences and possibilities of a long-term nature.

Involve others in the organization

It is a good idea to assist other people in your organization, so that they can feel they are part and parcel of the general mission. Once you assist them, they are bound to feel part of the overall strategy, and you accomplish this by frequently discussing that strategy and involving everyone else the best you can.

Pause and review

The reason you want to pause is to review the situation or the challenge, and try and assess it from a different perspective. If you are a manager, for instance, you may wish to try looking at the situation from the perspective of an employee, a supplier, a customer, your banker, and so on.

Analyze your main competitor(s)

For you to beat your competitors you need to, first of all, understand them. You need to know how they go about sourcing their materials, for example, how they manage their distribution network, and such other matters. In fact, what experts offer as advice is that you create a detailed profile of your competitors, and then you proceed to share it with members of your team. One important point you need to note is the need to rely on real credible information, as opposed to depending on anecdotes you have heard from other people.

Engage suppositions

What is meant here is the need to ask 'what if' to yourself, where you suppose a what if situation and not what the circumstances are today. So, you can for example, ask – Suppose we were to do this in this regard, how would our competitors behave in response? What impact would their response have on our distributors or even on our suppliers? Suppose there is something we have missed out in our analysis and evaluation?

Compare data from different sectors

You need to diversify your sources of data, so that you also include those areas that are outside of your sector. In the process, you could analyze businesses outside your industry, and have a look at what it is that they do right in order to succeed. In short, for you to succeed in your sector, you do not have to assess only what is happening close home. Success in other industries can also be helpful. Once you notice some good practice in that industry, you can adopt it, and when you notice methods the other industry relies on to circumvent hitches, you can adopt those ones too.

Temporarily focus elsewhere
For some time, take your focus elsewhere and think about something else that is not related to your business. Thinking about different things, different habitats, different styles of doing things and so on, is stimulating to the mind. And you could even keep it simple and just do something very easy, like walking outside your premises. During such walks, all you need to do is enjoy the view as you walk around, listen to the natural sounds of birds and swinging branches, even as you imbibe the nice scents from the vegetation in the environment.

Allow your mind to wander freely, and even let yourself do a bit of daydreaming. It will surprise you at how much learning you can do, and how clear your perspectives can be, when you shift your focus from the critical thinking or from implementation thinking mode. It actually helps to do this periodically.

Your human brain happens to be a tool that is very powerful in the leadership process, and it works much better when you utilize the entire list of five thinking modes.

Thinking versus Feeling

Which one comes first – feeling or thinking? Many people are likely to say that feelings come first. However, experts in cognitive psychology hold the premise that what you feel is a result of what you think. So, yes – according to these psychologists, thinking precedes feeling. That is why someone can throw an insult at you and yet your emotions do not change for the worse.

This is an interesting topic, and there is even a quote from Jean de la Bruyere, saying *"Life is a tragedy for those who feel, and a comedy for those who think."* And while this quote may sound kind of radical, it provides good food for thought. You cannot fail to see how the quote ignites people into taking responsibility for their attitude, while at the same time enjoying the freedom to pick their mood, their thoughts as well as their perspectives.

It is liberating to know you have the liberty to choose what you think, and also the freedom to direct the way you think. In the same vein, you have the power to control many circumstances of your life, to improve your processes of decision making, and to generally lead lives that are more productive. Mark you in so doing you will not be trying to downplay your feelings or even your emotions, but it only means you are better placed to manage your abilities, and to balance your cognitive abilities.

Nature of a Critical Thinking Mindset

Do you know you need to be in a certain mindset to be able

to think critically? Some of the things that show you have a critical thinking mindset include:

- Relying on your reasoning as opposed to your emotions

- Evaluating a wide range of perspectives

- Maintaining a mind that is open to different interpretations

- Accepting fresh evidence and explanations, as well as findings

- Having willingness to reassess the information you have

- Ability to put aside your personal biases as well as prejudices

- Ability to put into consideration every reasonable possibility

- Ability and willingness to avoid judgments that are hasty

Even after learning the attributes you need, and the mindset that you need, you still require some time to practice, before you can master the problem solving skills efficiently. Needless to say, you will be called upon to exercise perseverance.

How the Best Managers Make Decisions

Do you remember one thing you have learned in earlier chapters of this book regarding decision making? Chances are you remember more than one thing, but what you can look forward to reading in this particular chapter are the best things to do when you want to become one of the best managers in the field. Remember decision-making is part of critical thinking and, as such, mastering it is a great way of enhancing your prowess in critical thinking.

Decision Making Tips the Best Managers Follow

How often do you make decisions? In reality, decision-making is a daily occurrence, and there are days you end up making more decisions than others. In fact, many are the times you make decisions under pressure. At such times, do you always make good decisions? Surely, it is not always. Sometimes, even when you make good decisions, you later realize you could have made better ones. So it is true to say you do not always make the best decisions under the circumstances.

However, it is possible to make the best decisions if you follow some easy tips provided here below. The reason you need to know specific strategies is so that you can avoid pitfalls that are common, and those that can hinder your progress in decision making. When you are able to make better decisions and faster ones, it helps you in taking advantage of available and emerging business opportunities.

Reframing the problem under scrutiny
Do you know the essence of reframing the problem? Well, for

one, when you reframe the problem, you are able to view the issue from a different angle, seeing any loopholes you may not have seen, and issues that are really not exactly problematic and do not require much adjusting. At the same time, it is relatively easy for you to balance the attention you are giving to every aspect of the problem. For more efficiency, try and identify three varying methods of viewing the problem.

Making decisions that are based on evidence

The acronym for decisions based on evidence is EBM. The aim of EBM is to utilize science based evidence in decision-making. This is as opposed to making decisions based on your personal instincts. Just like many other people, you may be using your personal judgment on issues, or basing the decisions you make on things or occurrences that are familiar. However, if you get down to analyzing situations, are all your previous experiences, or your experiences in different organizations, match the situation you are facing currently? Not necessarily...

Ways to Incorporate Your Evidence into Decision Making

The fact that you have the same evidence as someone else does not mean that both of you are going to necessarily use the evidence in the same way when trying to solve similar problems. Here below, you will find various ways that you can follow, in putting your evidence to use.

Support your decisions using performance data

You need to collect data that is most current, and ensure you have a complete package as far as the challenge at hand is concerned.

Practice challenging your own gut feeling
Going by your gut feeling means you are not trying to rely on any evidence whatsoever, but rather on what your feelings tell you. Now you are being called upon to calm down and engage your reasoning, taking time to look at tangible or credible evidence. That is what successful managers do. They sieve the information they have, trying to see if there is some objective evidence that can support their gut feelings.

Confirm evidence before taking up suggestion
Are you going to take up a suggestion just because someone has thrown it to you? Of course not! What you need to do is establish what the suggestion made is based upon, and then you decide if what you find is sufficient to make the suggestion helpful. As a basic necessity, the suggestion need to be data based.

Establish if the suggestion you have received has been used elsewhere, probably to enhance another organization's business strategy, and also find out how successful it was in that situation. Try and gauge that other organization's situation against your organization's position, and assess if the suggestion is likely to apply to your case. Very importantly, you need to establish that the data the suggestion is based on is current and also objective.

Make a point of challenging status quo
How many people look forward to finding something changed the next morning when they report to work? Actually, many people look forward to continuing where they left off the previous day. Even when the change implemented proves to be beneficial to those affected it is not always that

people are excited about it at the beginning. However, to be a great manager or decision maker, you need to be prepared to accept change. Many would rather they remained within their comfort zone.

The point you need to note here is that it does not always help to remain in your comfort zone. It should not be enough that you are comfortable with the approach you are using. What you need to ask is if the approach you normally follow is one you would identify for use today, if you were to choose. In challenging the status quo to see if you need to change your approach to things, you need to compare options, including the cost aspect and the issue of effort needed in each of the options you are evaluating.

A good example is marketing a product. If you were to choose a marketing tactic today, would you choose the one you are engaged in right now, or would you choose a different one? Would you frequent the trade shows you visit today, or would you attend different ones? Would you opt to continue with traditional ways of marketing your product, or would you put more emphasis to online marketing?

Incorporate an outsider's perspective
Do you think you are doing a good job in your organization, in your independent project, and so on? Your answer may be a yes or a no, but whatever it is, it will be a response emanating from your personal perspective. Why not seek the opinion of an outsider, someone who is likely to be neutral in the matter and someone who has no biases or prejudices in the topic at hand? That is a great way to confirm you are open minded, something that a successful manager must be.

The question is, are you going to change your stance when

you get feedback or an opinion from one outsider? No! You need to listen to a number of outsiders who are reliable, so that you can evaluate the issue from different valid perspectives.

Weigh your employees' opinions

Are you one of those employers who feel employees are there to work as per instructions and not to offer opinions? If so, you may wish to change that after seeing the benefits of listening to varying perspectives to an issue. Plain talk from your employees can be very helpful, and it could help you see reality you never get to see while seated behind your desk. This means if you listen to what your employees sincerely feel, you are likely to tailor your policies in a way that augurs well, not just for the employees, but also for the organization as a whole. What can you see as the implication here? Well, you are looking at a possible situation where your employees have an atmosphere that is conducive to airing their views, and where they can formally express their opinion without fearing intimidation even when the reality they are expressing is unpleasant.

Be sensitive to risk

You could call it being sensitive to risk, and you could also term it developing an eye for risk. The point here is that you need to be able to tell when there is obvious risk involved in the decision you are about to take, and if so, what magnitude that risk is. The question you need to be asking yourself is how you can tell when you are taking a risk. Of course, the signals for risk will be different in different industries, and so it is up to you to establish what the telltale signs are in your specific industry or even sector.

Conclusion

As you have already seen from the information in this book, , *"Critical Thinking: A Beginner's Guide To Critical Thinking, Better Decision Making and Problem Solving!"*, you have a brain that works virtually like a super computer. It is that brain that directs the way your body functions, and it is the same brain that determines how you tailor your life. It also has a great influence on who you are as an individual, what you actually do and even the proficiency with which you do it.

For that reason, it is very important that you maintain the health of your brain, because, in so doing, you are going to be better at decision-making. You will also be better placed to think logically, and to do things that have a positive impact on your life. Mark you, it does not mean that when you think in a logical manner you erode your emotions. It only means that you are able to let reason prevail over your feelings, making decisions that can be easily validated.

It is important to bear in mind the fact that your own brain is unique, and that it is more complicated than even that super-computer you have read about. In all ways, your brain happens to be one amazing organ whose health you cannot afford to ignore. You need to be protective of it, particularly seeing to it that it does not lose its elasticity. If your brain lost its elasticity, you would find yourself becoming complacent, and as you may guess, complacency is a poor ingredient in the process of critical thinking.

The advantage you have now is that you have learnt from this book what you need to do in terms of exercises, in order to keep your brain elastic and working in a logical manner.

And, as you have also seen, consistency is the way to go –
engaging in critical thinking at every opportune moment.

All the best, as you seek to improve your life through critical
thinking!

CPSIA information can be obtained
at www.ICGtesting.com
Printed in the USA
BVHW011217050419
544730BV00012B/98/P